THE  SHORTER CATECHISM

IN MODERN ENGLISH

by
Douglas Kelly
and
Philip Rollinson

with
Frederick T. Marsh
Thomas I. Rice III
A. Jerry Sheldon
Luder G. Whitlock, Jr.
William K. Wymond

Presbyterian and Reformed Publishing Company
Phillipsburg, New Jersey

Manufactured in the United States of America.

Library of Congress Cataloging-in-Publication Data

Westminster Assembly.
  The Westminster Shorter catechism in modern English.

  Summary: A modern English version of the Shorter Catechism
designed for the instruction of young people and their parents.
  1. Presbyterian Church—Catechisms—English.
2. Reformed Church—Catechisms—English.
[1. Presbyterian Church—Catechisms. 2. Reformed
Church—Catechisms] I. Kelly, Douglas, 1943-
II. Rollinson, Philip B. III. Marsh, Frederick T.
IV. Title.
BX9184.A4 1986   238'.52   86-22592
ISBN 0-87552-548-2

Preface

This is a precise, accurate rendering of the Westminster Shorter Catechism into modern English. After more than 300 years much of the language of the original is obsolete, obscure, and sometimes difficult to use and understand in the modern church. Churches committed to the Westminster standards will now be able to continue using the Shorter Catechism to instruct children and communicants.

Several laymen associated with First Presbyterian Church in Jackson, Mississippi, conceived of this project. Subsequently, a somewhat larger group of laymen within that church (The WestShor Group) generously agreed to underwrite the expenses of the project. To do the job, they hired a theologian at the Reformed Theological Seminary (Dr. Douglas Kelly) and a philologist at the University of South Carolina (Dr. Philip Rollinson). To review and refine the results, they assembled a committee of five who participated actively throughout the process of preparing this version.

Quotations from the Bible in this modern version of the Shorter Catechism are taken from *The Holy Bible:*

The WestShor Group

James N. Adams
John H. Bowen
B. F. Bracy
Charles C. Decker
Larry W. Edwards
Dean R. Fulghom
W. Boyd Massey, M.D.
James S. Overstreet
Joel G. Payne, Jr., M.D.
Edward B. Polk
Thomas I. Rice III
Stephen W. Rosenblatt
A. Jerry Sheldon
Rowan H. Taylor, Jr.
William L. Watson III
Dr. and Mrs. Luder G. Whitlock, Jr.

Westminster Translation Committee

Rev. Frederick T. Marsh
Thomas I. Rice III
A. Jerry Sheldon
Dr. Luder G. Whitlock, Jr.
Rev. William K. Wymond

The Shorter Catechism

Q. 1. What is man's primary purpose?
A. Man's primary purpose is to glorify God and to enjoy Him forever.

Q. 2. What authority from God directs us how to glorify and enjoy Him?
A. The only authority for glorifying and enjoying Him is the Bible, which is the word of God and is made up of the Old and New Testaments.

Q. 3. What does the Bible primarily teach?
A. The Bible primarily teaches what man must believe about God and what God requires of man.

Q. 4. What is God?
A. God is a spirit, Whose being, wisdom, power, holiness, justice, goodness, and truth are infinite, eternal, and unchangeable.

Q. 5. Is there more than one God?
A. There is only one, the living and true God.

Q. 6. How many persons are in the one God?
A. Three persons are in the one God, the Father, the Son, and the Holy Spirit. These three are one God, the same in substance and equal in power and glory.

Q. 7. What are the decrees of God?
A. The decrees of God are His eternal plan based on the purpose of His will, by which, for His own glory, He has foreordained everything that happens.

Q. 8. How does God carry out His decrees?
A. God carries out His decrees in creation and providence.

Q. 9. What is creation?
A. Creation is God's making everything out of nothing by His powerful word in six days—and all very good.

Q. 10. How did God create man?
A. God created man, male and female, in His own image and in knowledge, righteousness, and holiness, to rule over the other creatures.

Q. 11. What is God's providence?
A. God's providence is His completely holy, wise, and powerful preserving and governing every creature and every action.

Q. 12. What did God's providence specifically do for man whom He created?
A. After the creation God made a covenant with man to give him life, if he perfectly obeyed; God told him

not to eat from the tree of knowledge of good and evil or he would die.

Q. 13. Did our first parents remain as they were created?

A. Left to the freedom of their own wills, our first parents sinned against God and fell from their original condition.

Q. 14. What is sin?

A. Sin is disobeying or not conforming to God's law in any way.

Q. 15. By what sin did our first parents fall from their original condition?

A. Our first parents' sin was eating the forbidden fruit.

Q. 16. Did all mankind fall in Adam's first disobedience?

A. Since the covenant was made not only for Adam but also for his natural descendants, all mankind sinned in him and fell with him in his first disobedience.

Q. 17. What happened to man in the fall?

A. Man fell into a condition of sin and misery.

Q. 18. What is sinful about man's fallen condition?

A. The sinfulness of that fallen condition is twofold. First, in what is commonly called original sin, there is the guilt of Adam's first sin with its lack of original righteousness and the corruption of his whole nature. Second are all the specific acts of disobedience that come from original sin.

Q. 19. What is the misery of man's fallen condition?

A. By their fall all mankind lost fellowship with God and brought His anger and curse on themselves. They are therefore subject to all the miseries of this life, to death itself, and to the pains of hell forever.

Q. 20. Did God leave all mankind to die in sin and misery?

A. From all eternity and merely because it pleased Him God chose some to have everlasting life. These He freed from sin and misery by a covenant of grace and brought them to salvation by a redeemer.

Q. 21. Who is the redeemer of God's chosen ones?

A. The only redeemer of God's chosen is the Lord Jesus Christ, the eternal Son of God, Who became man. He was and continues to be God and man in two distinct natures and one person forever.

Q. 22. How did Christ, the Son of God, become man?

A. Christ, the Son of God, became man by assuming a real body and a reasoning soul. He was conceived by the power of the Holy Spirit in the womb of the Virgin Mary, who gave birth to Him; yet He was sinless.

Q. 23. How is Christ our redeemer?

A. As our redeemer, Christ is a prophet, priest, and king in both His humiliation and His exaltation.

Q. 24. How is Christ a prophet?

A. As a prophet, Christ reveals the will of God to us for our salvation by His word and Spirit.

Q. 25. How is Christ a priest?

A. As a priest, Christ offered Himself up once as a sacrifice for us to satisfy divine justice and to reconcile us to God, and He continually intercedes for us.

Q. 26. How is Christ a king?

A. As a king, Christ brings us under His power, rules and defends us, and restrains and conquers all His and all our enemies.

Q. 27. How was Christ humiliated?

A. Christ was humiliated: by being born as a man and born into a poor family; by being made subject to the law and suffering the miseries of this life, the anger of God, and the curse of death on the cross; and by being buried and remaining under the power of death for a time.

Q. 28. How is Christ exalted?

A. Christ is exalted by His rising from the dead on the third day, His going up into heaven, His sitting at the right hand of God the Father, and His coming to judge the world at the last day.

Q. 29. How are we made to take part in the redemption Christ bought?

A. We take part in the redemption Christ bought when the Holy Spirit effectively applies it to us.

Q. 30. How does the Holy Spirit apply to us the redemption Christ bought?

A. The Spirit applies to us the redemption Christ bought by producing faith in us and so uniting us to

Christ in our effective calling.

Q. 31. What is effective calling?

A. Effective calling is the work of God's Spirit, Who convinces us that we are sinful and miserable, Who enlightens our minds in the knowledge of Christ, and Who renews our wills. This is how He persuades and makes us able to receive Jesus Christ, Who is freely offered to us in the gospel.

Q. 32. What benefits do those who are effectively called share in this life?

A. In this life those who are effectively called share justification, adoption, sanctification, and the other benefits that either go with or come from them.

Q. 33. What is justification?

A. Justification is the act of God's free grace by which He pardons all our sins and accepts us as righteous in His sight. He does so only because He counts the righteousness of Christ as ours. Justification is received by faith alone.

Q. 34. What is adoption?

A. Adoption is the act of God's free grace by which we become His sons with all the rights and privileges of being His.

Q. 35. What is sanctification?

A. Sanctification is the work of God's free grace by which our whole person is made new in the image of God, and we are made more and more able to become dead to sin and alive to righteousness.

Q. 36. What benefits in this life go with or come from justification, adoption, and sanctification?

A. The benefits that in this life go with or come from justification, adoption, and sanctification are: the assurance of God's love, peace of conscience, joy in the Holy Spirit, and growing and persevering in grace to the end of our lives.

Q. 37. What benefits do believers receive from Christ when they die?

A. When believers die, their souls are made perfectly holy and immediately pass into glory. Their bodies, which are still united to Christ, rest in the grave until the resurrection.

Q. 38. What benefits do believers receive from Christ at the resurrection?

A. At the resurrection, believers, raised in glory, will be publicly recognized and declared not guilty on the day of judgment and will be made completely happy in the full enjoyment of God forever.

Q. 39. What does God require of man?

A. God requires man to obey His revealed will.

Q. 40. What rules did God first reveal for man to obey?

A. The rules He first revealed were the moral law.

Q. 41. Where is the moral law summarized?

A. The moral law is summarized in the ten commandments.

Q. 42. What is the essence of the ten commandments?

A. The essence of the ten commandments is to love the Lord our God with all our heart, with all our soul, with all our strength, and with all our mind, and to love everyone else as we love ourselves.

Q. 43. What introduces the ten commandments?
A. These words introduce the ten commandments: *I am the Lord your God, who brought you out of Egypt, out of the land of slavery.*

Q. 44. What does the introduction to the ten commandments teach us?
A. The introduction to the ten commandments teaches us that, because God is Lord and is our God and redeemer, we must keep all His commandments.

Q. 45. What is the first commandment?
A. The first commandment is: *You shall have no other gods before me.*

Q. 46. What does the first commandment require?
A. The first commandment requires us to know and recognize God as the only true God and our God, and to worship and glorify Him accordingly.

Q. 47. What does the first commandment forbid?
A. The first commandment forbids denying God or not worshipping and glorifying Him as the true God and our God. It also forbids giving worship and glory, which He alone deserves, to anyone or anything else.

Q. 48. What are we specifically taught in the first commandment by the words *before me*?

A. The words *before me* in the first commandment teach us that God, Who sees everything, notices and is very offended by the sin of having any other god.

Q. 49. What is the second commandment?

A. The second commandment is: *You shall not make for yourself an idol in the form of anything in heaven above or on the earth beneath or in the waters below. You shall not bow down to them or worship them; for I, the Lord your God, am a jealous God, punishing the children for the sin of the fathers to the third and fourth generation of those who hate me, but showing love to a thousand [generations] of those who love me and keep my commandments.*

Q. 50. What does the second commandment require?

A. The second commandment requires us to receive, respectfully perform, and preserve completely and purely all the regulations for religion and worship that God has established in His word.

Q. 51. What does the second commandment forbid?

A. The second commandment forbids our worshipping God with images or in any other way not established in His word.

Q. 52. What are the reasons for the second commandment?

A. The reasons for the second commandment are that God totally rules over us, that we belong to Him, and that He is eager to be worshipped correctly.

Q. 53. What is the third commandment?

A. The third commandment is: *You shall not misuse the name of the Lord your God, for the Lord will not hold anyone guiltless who misuses his name.*

Q. 54. What does the third commandment require?

A. The third commandment requires the holy and reverent use of God's names, titles, qualities, regulations, word, and works.

Q. 55. What does the third commandment forbid?

A. The third commandment forbids our treating as unholy or abusing anything God uses to make Himself known.

Q. 56. What is the reason for the third commandment?

A. The reason for the third commandment is that the Lord our God will not allow those who break this commandment to escape His righteous judgment, although they may escape punishment from men.

Q. 57. What is the fourth commandment?

A. The fourth commandment is: *Remember the Sabbath day by keeping it holy. Six days you shall labor and do all your work, but the seventh day is a Sabbath to the Lord your God. On it you shall not do any work, neither you, nor your son or daughter, nor your manservant or maidservant, nor your animals, nor the alien within your gates. For in six days the Lord made the heavens and the earth, the sea, and all that is in them, but he rested on the seventh day. Therefore the Lord blessed the Sabbath day and made it holy.*

Q. 58. What does the fourth commandment require?

A. The fourth commandment requires us to set apart to God the times He has established in His word—specifically one whole day out of every seven as a holy Sabbath to Him.

Q. 59. Which day of the week has God designated as the Sabbath?

A. From the beginning of the world until the resurrection of Christ God established the seventh day of the week as the Sabbath. From that time until the end of the world the first day of the week is the Christian Sabbath.

Q. 60. How do we keep the Sabbath holy?

A. We keep the Sabbath holy by resting the whole day from worldly affairs or recreations, even ones that are lawful on other days. Except for necessary works or acts of mercy we should spend all our time publicly and privately worshipping God.

Q. 61. What does the fourth commandment forbid?

A. The fourth commandment forbids failing to do or carelessly doing what we are supposed to do. It also forbids treating the day as unholy by loafing, by doing anything in itself sinful, or by unnecessary thinking, talking about, or working on our worldly affairs or recreations.

Q. 62. What are the reasons for the fourth commandment?

A. The reasons for the fourth commandment are these: God allows us six days of the week to take care of our own affairs; He claims the seventh day as His own; He set the example; and He blesses the Sabbath.

Q. 63. What is the fifth commandment?

A. The fifth commandment is: *Honor your father and your mother, so that you may live long in the land the Lord your God is giving you.*

Q. 64. What does the fifth commandment require?

A. The fifth commandment requires us to respect and treat others, whether above, below, or equal to us, as their position or our relationship to them demands.

Q. 65. What does the fifth commandment forbid?

A. The fifth commandment forbids being disrespectful to or not treating others as their position or relationship to us demands.

Q. 66. What is the reason for the fifth commandment?

A. The reason for the fifth commandment is the promise of long life and prosperity, if these glorify God and are for the good of those who obey this commandment.

Q. 67. What is the sixth commandment?

A. The sixth commandment is: *You shall not murder.*

Q. 68. What does the sixth commandment require?

A. The sixth commandment requires making every lawful effort to preserve one's own life and the lives of others.

Q. 69. What does the sixth commandment forbid?

A. The sixth commandment forbids taking one's own life or the lives of others unjustly or doing anything that leads to suicide or murder.

Q. 70. What is the seventh commandment?

A. The seventh commandment is: *You shall not commit adultery.*

Q. 71. What does the seventh commandment require?

A. The seventh commandment requires us and everyone else to keep sexually pure in heart, speech, and action.

Q. 72. What does the seventh commandment forbid?

A. The seventh commandment forbids thinking, saying, or doing anything sexually impure.

Q. 73. What is the eighth commandment?

A. The eighth commandment is: *You shall not steal.*

Q. 74. What does the eighth commandment require?

A. The eighth commandment requires that we lawfully acquire and increase our own and others' money and possessions.

Q. 75. What does the eighth commandment forbid?

A. The eighth commandment forbids anything that either does or may unjustly take away money or possessions from us or anyone else.

Q. 76. What is the ninth commandment?

A. The ninth commandment is: *You shall not give false*

testimony against your neighbor.

Q. 77. What does the ninth commandment require?
A. The ninth commandment requires us to tell the truth and to maintain and promote it and our own and others' reputations, especially when testifying.

Q. 78. What does the ninth commandment forbid?
A. The ninth commandment forbids anything that gets in the way of the truth or injures anyone's reputation.

Q. 79. What is the tenth commandment?
A. The tenth commandment is: *You shall not covet your neighbor's house. You shall not covet your neighbor's wife, or his manservant or maidservant, his ox or donkey, or anything that belongs to your neighbor.*

Q. 80. What does the tenth commandment require?
A. The tenth commandment requires us to be completely satisfied with our own status in life and to have a proper, loving attitude toward others and their possessions.

Q. 81. What does the tenth commandment forbid?
A. The tenth commandment forbids any dissatisfaction with what belongs to us, envy or grief at the success of others, and all improper desire for anything that belongs to someone else.

Q. 82. Can anyone perfectly keep the commandments of God?

A. Since the fall no ordinary man can perfectly keep the commandments of God in this life but breaks them every day in thought, word, and action.

Q. 83. Are all sins equally evil?
A. In the eyes of God some sins in themselves are more evil than others, and some are more evil because of the harm that results from them.

Q. 84. What does every sin deserve?
A. Every sin deserves God's anger and curse, both in this life and in the life to come.

Q. 85. What does God require from us to escape His anger and curse, which we deserve for our sin?
A. To escape God's anger and curse, which we deserve for our sin, God requires from us faith in Jesus Christ and repentance unto life along with diligent involvement in all the external ways Christ uses to bring us the benefits of redemption.

Q. 86. What is faith in Jesus Christ?
A. Faith in Jesus Christ is a saving grace, by which we receive and rest on Him alone for salvation, as He is offered to us in the gospel.

Q. 87. What is repentance unto life?
A. Repentance unto life is a saving grace, by which a sinner, being truly aware of his sinfulness, understands the mercy of God in Christ, grieves for and hates his sins, and turns from them to God, fully intending and striving for a new obedience.

Q. 88. What are the ordinary, external ways Christ uses to bring us the benefits of redemption?

A. The ordinary, external ways Christ uses to bring us the benefits of redemption are His regulations, particularly the word, sacraments, and prayer, all of which are made effective for the salvation of His chosen ones.

Q. 89. What makes the word effective for salvation?

A. The Spirit of God causes the reading and especially the preaching of the word to convince and convert sinners and to build them up in holiness and comfort through faith to salvation.

Q. 90. How is the word to be read and heard in order to become effective for salvation?

A. For the word to become effective for salvation, we must pay careful attention to it, prepare ourselves, and pray for understanding. We must also receive it with faith and love, treasure it in our hearts, and practice it in our lives.

Q. 91. How do the sacraments become effective means of salvation?

A. The sacraments become effective means of salvation, not because of any special power in them or in the people who administer them, but rather by the blessing of Christ and the working of His Spirit in those who receive them by faith.

Q. 92. What is a sacrament?

A. A sacrament is a holy regulation established by Christ, in which Christ and the benefits of the new covenant are represented, sealed, and applied to believers by physical signs.

Q. 93. What are the sacraments of the New Testament?
A. The sacraments of the New Testament are baptism and the Lord's Supper.

Q. 94. What is baptism?
A. The sacrament of baptism is a washing with water in the name of the Father, the Son, and the Holy Spirit, which is a sign and seal that we are joined to Christ, that we receive the benefits of the covenant of grace, and that we are engaged to be the Lord's.

Q. 95. Who should be baptized?
A. Those who are not members of churches should not be baptized until they have publicly stated that they believe in Christ and will obey Him, but the infant children of church members should be baptized.

Q. 96. What is the Lord's Supper?
A. The Lord's Supper is a sacrament in which bread and wine are given and received as Christ directed to proclaim His death. Those who receive the Lord's Supper in the right way share in His body and blood with all His benefits, not physically but by faith, and become spiritually stronger and grow in grace.

Q. 97. What is the right way to receive the Lord's Supper?
A. The right way to receive the Lord's Supper is to examine whether we discern the Lord's body,

whether our faith feeds on Him, and whether we have repentance, love, and a new obedience—so that we may not come in the wrong way and eat and drink judgment on ourselves.

Q. 98. What is prayer?

A. Prayer is offering our desires to God in the name of Christ for things that agree with His will, confessing our sins, and thankfully recognizing His mercies.

Q. 99. How does God direct us to pray?

A. The whole word of God, but especially the Lord's prayer, which Christ taught His disciples, directs our prayers.

Q. 100. What does the beginning of the Lord's prayer teach us?

A. The beginning of the Lord's prayer (*Our Father in heaven*) teaches us to draw near to God with completely holy reverence and confidence, as children to a father who is able and ready to help us. It also teaches that we should pray with and for others.

Q. 101. For what do we pray in the first request?

A. In the first request (*hallowed be your name*) we pray that God will enable us and others to glorify Him in everything He uses to make Himself known and that He will work out everything to His own glory.

Q. 102. For what do we pray in the second request?

A. In the second request (*your kingdom come*) we pray that Satan's kingdom may be destroyed, that the kingdom of grace may be advanced, with ourselves

and others brought into and kept in it, and that the
kingdom of glory may come quickly.

Q. 103. For what do we pray in the third request?

A. In the third request (*your will be done on earth as it
is in heaven*) we pray that by His grace God would
make us have the capability and the will to know,
obey, and submit to His will in everything, as the
angels do in heaven.

Q. 104. For what do we pray in the fourth request?

A. In the fourth request (*Give us today our daily bread*)
we pray that we may receive an adequate amount of
the good things in this life as a free gift of God and
that with them we may enjoy His blessing.

Q. 105. For what do we pray in the fifth request?

A. In the fifth request (*Forgive us our debts, as we also
have forgiven our debtors*), encouraged by God's
grace, which makes it possible for us sincerely to forgive others, we pray that for Christ's sake God
would freely pardon all our sins.

Q. 106. For what do we pray in the sixth request?

A. In the sixth request (*And lead us not into temptation,
but deliver us from the evil one*) we pray that God
would either keep us from being tempted to sin or
support and deliver us when we are tempted.

**Q. 107. What does the conclusion of the Lord's prayer
teach us?**

A. The conclusion of the Lord's prayer (*for yours is the
kingdom and the power and the glory forever*)

teaches us to be encouraged only by God in our prayers and to praise Him by acknowledging that kingdom, power, and glory are His. To show that we want to be heard and have confidence that we are, we say *Amen.*